CONTENTS

KU-023-989

INTRODUCTION

The ancient Greeks were one of the most inventive peoples in history. In their cities they invented the art of politics, creating the first states in which citizens actually ruled themselves. They had some of the world's first historians and scientists. They were fine craftsmen and poets. Theatre was also invented by the Greeks. In short, the Greeks can be seen as the founders of much of modern European life.

The Greeks reached the height of their civilization 2,500 years ago. This was the period when Athens was the most successful city in Greece and famous buildings such as the Parthenon were built there.

FINDING OUT MORE

Remains of the Greeks, in particular their temples, can be found in modern Greece, Turkey and Italy. Much of their pottery and sculpture can be seen in museums throughout the world.

A lot can be learned about the Greeks from looking at the pictures on their fine pottery and from reading their famous war stories such as the siege of Troy.

HOW TO USE THIS BOOK

This book explores and explains the world of the ancient Geeks. Each double-page spread looks at a particular aspect of life in Greece, building up a fascinating picture of this important civilization.

INTRODUCTION

Concise yet highly informative, this text introduces the reader to the topics covered in the spread. This broad coverage is complemented by more detailed exploration of particular points in the numerous captions.

INSET ARTWORKS

Subjects that help to explain particular points are shown in inset along with an explanation of their significance.

SPOTLIGHTS

A series of illustrations at the bottom of each page encourages the reader to look out for objects from ancient Greece that can be found in museums.

TEMPLES

A temple was b a god. Cities con othe to build the decorated temples

There would be the god or goddess temple and often th would be stored the picture is a reconstr Parthenon, which wa Athens. Not all temp cities. Some would be remote spots.

Doric

ARCHITECTURE

Greek temples are found in two s Doric on the mainland and in the cities of Italy, and Ionic in the citie coast of what is now Turkey. Notic difference in the decoration of the c

| ✓ | LOOK OUT FOR THESE |

IONIC CA
The top of a col called the capita capitals with the rounded volutes (spiralled scroll tops) are eas spot. The Ionians built some of the largest temples

24

SPOTLIGHTS

THE ANCIENT GREEKS

Written by Charles Freeman

SIMON & SCHUSTER
YOUNG BOOKS

ACKNOWLEDGMENTS

Illustrated by
Bruce Hogarth - David Lewis Management: 34-35, 40-41, 42-43
Maltings Partnership: 8-9, 10-11, 14-15, 19, 20, 24-25
Tony Smith: 12-13, 22-23, 26-27, 30-31, 38-39
Clive Spong - Linden Artists: Spotlights 8-43
Mark Viney - Allied Artists: 16-17, 18-19, 28-29, 32-33, 36-37

First published in 1994 by
Simon & Schuster Young Books
Simon & Schuster Limited
Campus 400
Maylands Avenue
Hemel Hempstead
Herts HP2 7EZ

Planned and produced by
Andromeda Oxford Limited
11-15 The Vineyard
Abingdon
Oxon OX14 3PX

Copyright © Andromeda Oxford Limited 1994

ISBN 0-7500-1565-9
Printed in Italy by Graphicom SRL

HEADING

The subject matter of each spread is clearly identified by a heading prominently displayed in the top left-hand corner.

DETAILED INFORMATION

From the building of their extraordinary temples to the everyday life of Greek families, the reader is given a wealth of information to help understand the ancient Greeks.

ILLUSTRATIONS

High quality, full colour artworks bring the world of the ancient Greeks to life. Each spread is packed with visual information.

REFERENCE TAB

Each group of subjects is keyed with a special colour to the contents page of the book so that different sections can be found quickly and easily.

PANATHENAEA
The main festival to Athena was held every year. It was called the Panathenaea, and included a great procession.

PEDIMENT
Legends were carved on to the pediment, which was the triangular upper part of the wall, close to the roof.

TREASURE STORE
The Athenians kept the money collected from cities in their empire inside the temple.

COLUMNS
Greek temples were always surrounded by columns. Those of the Parthenon were in the finest marble, brought from the nearby quarries of Pentele.

STATUE OF ATHENA
The massive statue of Athena in the Parthenon was sculpted by Phidias. The outside of the wooden statue was coated in gold, and Athena's skin was made of ivory.

CELLA
The cella housed the statue to Athena. There was only light from one door so the statue must have looked rather frightening.

PLE SCULPTURE
ure comes from pediments of the eus at Olympia. y man who er to see ough lly

FRIEZE
Greeks carved pictures on to their walls, called friezes. This one is on the inner wall of the Parthenon. It is the great procession of the Panathenaeic festival.

CARYATID PORCH
This porch, with its columns in the shape of women, was part of an ancient temple to Athena called the Erechtheion.

THE MYCENAEANS AND HOMER

The first Greeks were called the Mycenaeans. They ruled southern Greece from 1600-1200 BC. Mycenae was their most important city. The Mycenaeans were warriors who set out from their fortified cities for the Mediterranean, looking for metals such as copper, tin and gold. Their civilization collapsed about 1200 BC. Their adventures were told by the poet Homer in his famous poems the *Iliad* and the *Odyssey*.

CITADEL
Mycenaean chiefs lived in fortified hilltop citadels. Each chieftain controlled the land around this, and traded its produce, pottery and weapons. The chieftains would join together to carry out raids overseas.

PALACE OF PYLOS
Homer wrote of the great palace of the Mycenaean king, Nestor of Pylos. This is a reconstruction of its throne room. It was burned down by raiders in about 1200 BC, but archaeologists uncovered its remains.

LOOK OUT FOR THESE

■ **POT**
The Mycenaeans were fine potters. This drinking cup, with its decoration of flowers, was found in a tomb. It dates from the 13th century BC.

■ **MASK**
This gold death mask of a warrior was one of the most spectacular finds in the graves at Mycenae. It dates from about 1550 BC.

■ **LIBATION BOOT**
This is a pottery boot from which offerings called libations would be poured to the gods.

8

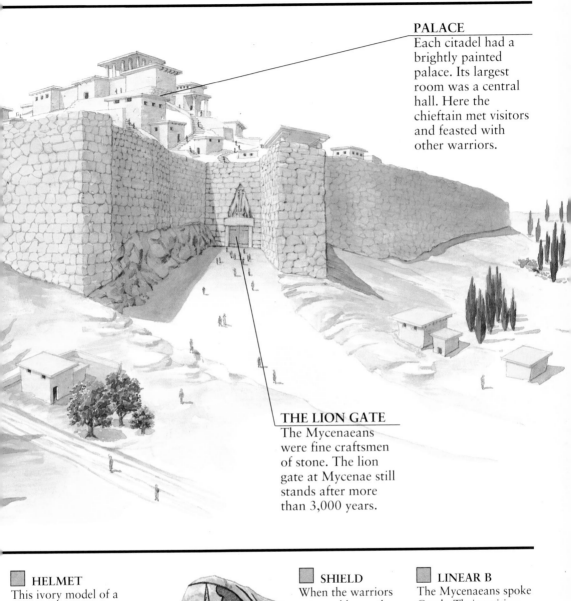

PALACE

Each citadel had a brightly painted palace. Its largest room was a central hall. Here the chieftain met visitors and feasted with other warriors.

THE LION GATE

The Mycenaeans were fine craftsmen of stone. The lion gate at Mycenae still stands after more than 3,000 years.

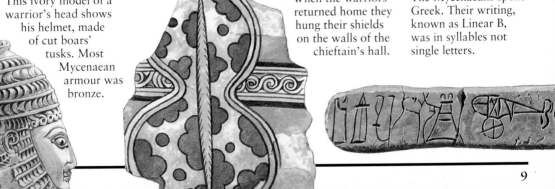

HELMET

This ivory model of a warrior's head shows his helmet, made of cut boars' tusks. Most Mycenaean armour was bronze.

SHIELD

When the warriors returned home they hung their shields on the walls of the chieftain's hall.

LINEAR B

The Mycenaeans spoke Greek. Their writing, known as Linear B, was in syllables not single letters.

GREEK SETTLEMENTS

When the Mycenaean civilization collapsed, Greeks scattered across the Aegean. By the 9th century BC, Greeks had settled across mainland Greece and in what is now southern Turkey and Cyprus. Greek traders then began trading with rich civilizations of the east.

By 750 BC the Greeks had also moved to the south coast of Italy in search of iron, and later began settling there. By the 6th century BC there were Greek settlements throughout the Mediterranean and Black Sea, and Greeks were mingling with many native peoples – Celts, Etruscans in Italy, and the wild Scythians of the Black Sea coast. Each settlement had its own system of government. In Egypt, Greek traders were given their own trading post, Naucratis. They brought silver and oil to exchange for corn.

ITALY
The Greeks settled in southern Italy and Sicily after 750 BC. These settlements became some of the richest cities in the Greek world.

CELTS

ETRUSCANS

ITALY

Pithecu

PHOENICIANS
These seafaring peoples also settled across the Mediterranean. They became rivals of the Greeks.

Greek homeland 1100-750 BC

The first colonies 750-700 BC

New Greek settlements 700-580 BC

The Phoenicians – rivals to the Greeks

LOOK OUT FOR THESE

KOUROI
Kouroi were life-size male statues often standing over a grave. Their design was influenced by the east and Egypt.

POT
Corinth was the most powerful Greek city of the 7th century BC. It had a fine position between the east and west and was a major ship building centre. Its pottery, often painted with animals and plants from the east, is found throughout the Mediterranean.

Black Sea

Al Mina

CYPRUS

IONIAN GREEKS

Aegean Sea

GREECE

Athens

Corinth
Mycenae

Mediterranean Sea

Naucratis

EGYPT

SICILY

Mediterranean
Sea

AFRICA

EUBOEA
It was sailors from Euboea who first traded with the east and then made the first Greek settlements to the west of Greece.

THE LANDING
Each expedition had a leader. His job was to choose the best site for a new settlement. The settlers often had to fight to get ashore and to win land for themselves.

CAULDRON
Bronze cauldrons were given as dedications to the gods. Over 500 have been found at Olympia, the site of the Olympic games. Craftsmen decorated them with exotic animals copied from the east. These animals are griffins.

SHIPWRECK
The Mediterranean can be a stormy sea and shipwrecks on its rocky coasts were common. Some shipwrecks have been found by modern archaeologists.

THE LAND OF GREECE

Greece is not a rich farming land. There are many mountains and there is too little rain in the hot summers. Farming had to take place on the plains or on terraced hills. Barley was the main cereal crop because it needed less water than wheat. Olives and vines also grew well and olive oil and wine were sold abroad in return for more grain. Sheep and goats grazed on the dry mountains.

Farmers' plots were small. When a farmer died his plot would be divided among his sons. One result was that the plots became even smaller and many Greeks could not survive on the land. They were forced to find new homes overseas.

Greece had very few metals, although there was iron. This could be used for agricultural tools and weapons.

PLOUGHING
The soil was ploughed often to help it hold the rain. Sowing took place in December with the harvest in May.

LOOK OUT FOR THESE

PLOUGH TEAM
The wooden ploughs cut a line through the soil. The farmer then had to break up the soil by hand.
Oxen were prized possessions as they saved much backbreaking work.

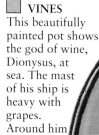

VINES
This beautifully painted pot shows the god of wine, Dionysus, at sea. The mast of his ship is heavy with grapes. Around him dolphins play in the water.

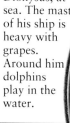

VINEYARDS
Vines were grown on terraces cut into the hillsides.

OLIVE GATHERING
Olive oil was one of the main exports of ancient Greece. The olive trees grew well in the dry soil and were often planted among the barley.

ANIMALS
These painted figures of a pig and hare show the pleasure Greeks took in animals.

DEMETER
Demeter was the goddess of crops such as wheat and barley. She was prayed to when the seed was planted. When the crop was gathered in, a great harvest festival was held in her honour.

FISH
Fresh fish was a welcome extra food. Here a fishmonger cuts one up.

THE CITY STATE – ATHENS

From the 8th century BC Greeks began to build cities. They were often built around a large rock to make them easier to defend. Greeks were proud of their cities which had many fine buildings.

Athens was surrounded by the plains of Attica which provided food and silver mines, and gave the city wealth to trade and to build warships. By 490 BC, when the Persians invaded Greece, it was the richest and most powerful Mediterranean city and was able to lead the fight against the Persians.

HOUSING
Athenian houses were not grand. The walls were of unbaked brick or timber, roofed with clay tiles. Athenian women normally stayed inside the home.

THE AGORA
The Agora was the market place. It was surrounded by many fine buildings, including stoas – long, open buildings with columns – where men discussed their business and ideas.

LOOK OUT FOR THESE

COINS
Most Greek cities used coins by 500 BC. This silver four drachma piece has Athena on one side and an owl, the symbol of Athens, on the other.

POTTERY
By 500 BC Athenian pottery was the finest in the Greek world. It usually had red paintings on a black background.

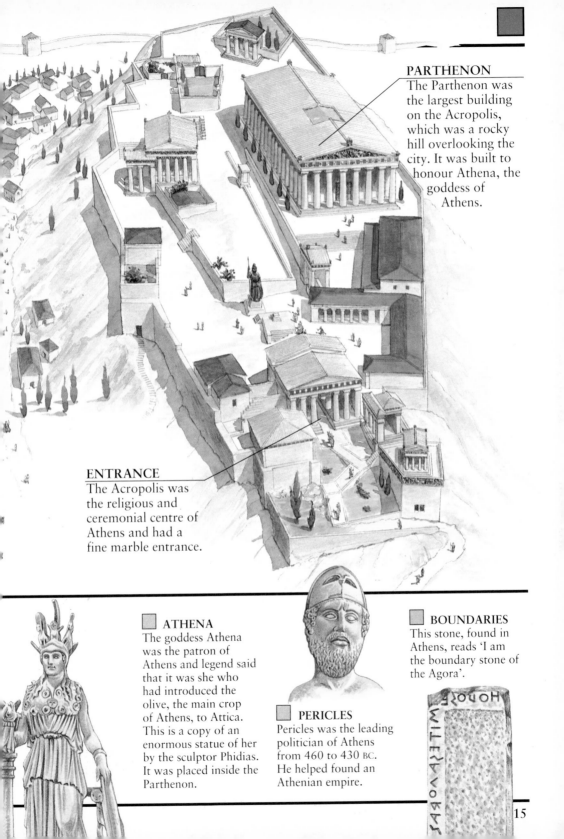

PARTHENON
The Parthenon was the largest building on the Acropolis, which was a rocky hill overlooking the city. It was built to honour Athena, the goddess of Athens.

ENTRANCE
The Acropolis was the religious and ceremonial centre of Athens and had a fine marble entrance.

ATHENA
The goddess Athena was the patron of Athens and legend said that it was she who had introduced the olive, the main crop of Athens, to Attica. This is a copy of an enormous statue of her by the sculptor Phidias. It was placed inside the Parthenon.

PERICLES
Pericles was the leading politician of Athens from 460 to 430 BC. He helped found an Athenian empire.

BOUNDARIES
This stone, found in Athens, reads 'I am the boundary stone of the Agora'.

DEMOCRACY

One of the major achievements of Athens was to involve its citizens in the running of its affairs. This system of goverment is known as democracy – rule by the people. In Athens, in fact, only men over 20 were classed as citizens and could vote. There were no votes for women, children, foreigners or the many slaves who lived in the city.

Every year, about 700 posts could be filled by citizens. They ranged from generals and treasurers to the keeper of the prison and street cleaners. All except the generals were selected for a year at a time by drawing lots, from men over 30 years of age.

Citizens could become jurors in trials, deciding whether an accused person was guilty or innocent.

ASSEMBLY
The Assembly met on the Pnyx, a hill in Athens, about 40 times a year. As many as 8,000 citizens could attend.

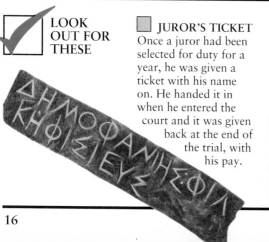

LOOK OUT FOR THESE

JUROR'S TICKET
Once a juror had been selected for duty for a year, he was given a ticket with his name on. He handed it in when he entered the court and it was given back at the end of the trial, with his pay.

WATER CLOCK
The speeches in trials were limited by the time which it took for water to run out from a pottery bowl.

BALLOTS
At the end of a trial jurors would vote on whether the accused was guilty or innocent. A solid ballot dropped in a box would mean innocent.

A CITIZEN'S VIEW

Meetings of the Assembly began early in the morning and could continue until dark. They were often rowdy. Sometimes decisions made in the heat of the debate were overturned the next day when emotions were calmer. Votes were taken by a show of hands.

DEBATES

Every month the Assembly discussed the city's defence and the state of its corn reserves.

DAY TO DAY RUNNING OF THE CITY

In between meetings of the Assembly, 50 citizens were on call day and night for a month at a time. They lived in a circular building, the Tholos, on the corner of the Agora.

ANTI-TYRANNY

The stone tablet below depicts the law that pardoned anyone who had killed a tyrant.

OSTRAKA

Athenians could exile citizens by writing their names on pieces of broken pottery called ostraka.

JUROR PICKING

If too many jurors turned up for a case, those who were to stay were selected by this ingenious machine.

THE CITY AT WAR

Because most Greek cities were short of land and food, they would often fight with each other. Battles would take place at set times of the year when men were not needed to work in the fields. It was considered very unfair to attack at other times. Soldiers had shields and spears. Battles were fought by both sides pushing, shoving and jabbing at each other until one army gave way and fled. Usually not many men were killed.

In 490 BC when the Persians invaded Greece, the Athenian army faced them on the plain of Marathon to the north of the city. To everyone's surprise, they pushed the Persians back towards the sea. A story says a runner raced back to Athens with the good news. This inspired the Marathon race.

PHALANX
The soldiers fought linked together in phalanxes (rows of men), probably about eight deep. The soldiers had to be well trained to hold a strong line together in the heat of the battle.

WEAPONS
The main fighting weapon was a wooden spear tipped with iron. It was used to prod an enemy until he was wounded, or turned and ran.

LOOK OUT FOR THESE

BURIAL MOUND
Only 192 Athenians died in the great victory at Marathon. They were buried in a huge mound which can still be seen on the battlefield today.

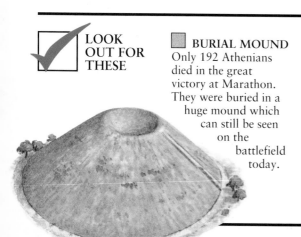

HOPLITE
The Greek name for the shield was 'hoplon' and the Greek soldier was usually called a hoplite.

WEAPONS FROM MARATHON
This sword and spear and arrow heads are from the Marathon battlefield. They show that there were archers as well as infantry.

MARATHON

This plan shows the battlefield of Marathon. The Athenians and their allies pushed the Persians back towards their ships, killing over 6,000 of them.

MARATHON 490 BC

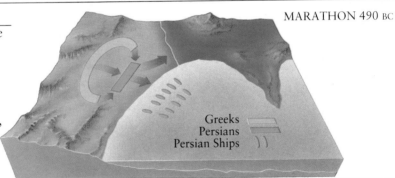

Greeks
Persians
Persian Ships

■ **ARMOUR**

The soldiers wore breastplates, helmets and greaves to protect their legs. Their shields were carefully packed away until needed. This vase painting shows a boy bringing a shield in ready for use.

■ **CAVALRY**

Cavalry existed but were not often used against hoplites because the riders did not have stirrups and could easily be pushed off their horses.

NAVAL WARFARE

The Greeks had always been good seamen and some of the cities had their own navies with warships called triremes. The trireme had three banks of oars. It needed about 170 men to row it. It did not carry artillery, and there were 30 armed men on board at the most. In battle, the trireme would crash head on into the weakest part of the enemy's ship – its side. The ship's crew had to make sure that the side of their ship was not exposed to attack.

One of the great Athenian naval victories was at Salamis in 480 BC. The Persians had invaded Greece with a large navy. The Athenians managed to lure the Persian ships into narrow water and destroyed them.

SALAMIS

This map shows what might have happened at the battle of Salamis. The Persians, with their allies the Phoenicians, sailed between the island of Salamis and the mainland and the Greeks attacked from the side. The Persians had no room to turn around or escape.

PERSIAN SHIPS

The Persians had soldiers ready to board the Greek ships but they were unable to get close enough.

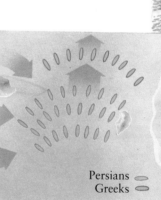

Persians ⬭
Greeks ⬭

LOOK OUT FOR THESE

 **TRIREME**

A trireme similar to ones built by the Greeks has been reconstructed and rowed. This has shown us that it must have been difficult to hear orders above the noise of the sea. A top speed of 16km an hour was possible.

TRIREME

The trireme was a war machine with no living space on board. It was usually beached at night.

POSITION OF ROWERS

The rowers in a trireme sat above each other. They had to avoid hitting each other's oars.

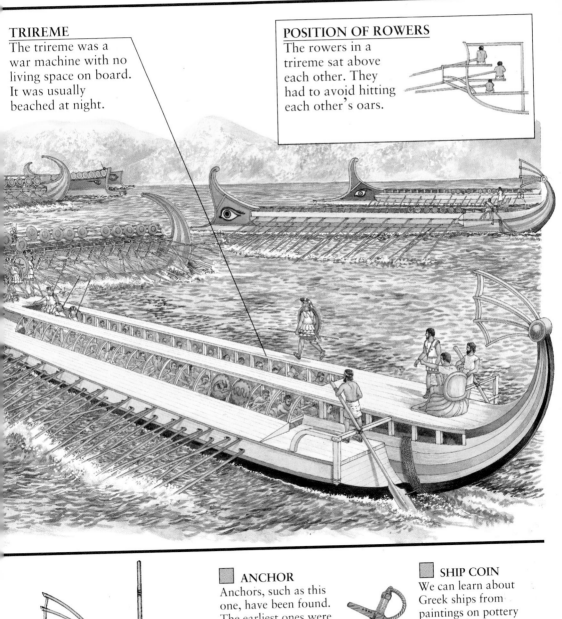

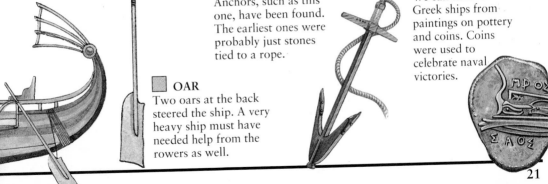

ANCHOR

Anchors, such as this one, have been found. The earliest ones were probably just stones tied to a rope.

OAR

Two oars at the back steered the ship. A very heavy ship must have needed help from the rowers as well.

SHIP COIN

We can learn about Greek ships from paintings on pottery and coins. Coins were used to celebrate naval victories.

RELIGION AND THE GODS

For the Greeks the gods were powerful figures who could either harm or help human beings. They were best approached through sacrifices. These were offerings of animals or wine through which the people hoped to win their favour. The gods would also give advice at oracles such as the famous one at Delphi. Here a priestess would give the god Apollo's answer to any questions asked by visitors.

The most important gods were those whom the Greeks believed lived on Mount Olympus in the north of Greece. They included Zeus the supreme god, Hera his wife, Aphrodite goddess of love, and Poseidon the god of earthquakes and the sea.

PROCESSION
Processions were colourful and noisy occasions, with lots of music. Young and old Greeks, as well as foreigners, each had their own place in the procession and brought their own offerings.

LOOK OUT FOR THESE

ZEUS
Zeus was the father of the gods and the most powerful. His throne was on Mount Olympus. He was god of the sky and storms, and when it rained people would say 'Zeus is raining'. If he was angry he could harm humans.

ATHENA
Athena was a war goddess. Athenians believed she had introduced olives to their city.

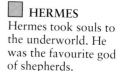
HERMES
Hermes took souls to the underworld. He was the favourite god of shepherds.

BURNT OFFERINGS

Fire was an important part of the sacrifice. The sacrificed animals were often burnt or cooked on the altar.

BEASTS

Oxen, goats, sheep or pigs were among the commonest animals sacrificed. They were killed with a sacred knife.

PRIESTS

Priests and priestesses made sure the sacrifice was carried out correctly.

APHRODITE

Aphrodite, goddess of love, was born from the sea. People prayed to her that their love would be returned by those they loved. This sculpture shows the birth of Aphrodite.

POSEIDON

Poseidon rode in his golden chariot across the waves, shipwrecking those who offended him.

APOLLO

Apollo, a god with youth and energy, was the god of music and also of healing. He gave advice at his oracle in Delphi.

TEMPLES

A temple was built as a home for a god. Cities competed with each other to build the largest and best decorated temples.

There would be a large statue of the god or goddess inside the temple and often the city treasure would be stored there. This picture is a reconstruction of the Parthenon, which was a temple in Athens. Not all temples were in cities. Some would be built in remote spots.

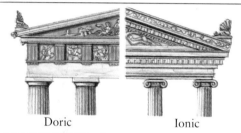

Doric   Ionic

ARCHITECTURE
Greek temples are found in two styles: Doric on the mainland and in the Greek cities of Italy, and Ionic in the cities on the coast of what is now Turkey. Notice the difference in the decoration of the columns.

PANATHENAEA
The main festival to Athena was held every year. It was called the Panathenaea, and included a great procession.

PEDIMENT
Legends were carved on to the pediment, which was the triangular upper part of the wall, close to the roof.

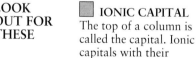

LOOK OUT FOR THESE

IONIC CAPITAL
The top of a column is called the capital. Ionic capitals with their rounded volutes (spiralled scroll tops) are easy to spot. The Ionians built some of the largest temples.

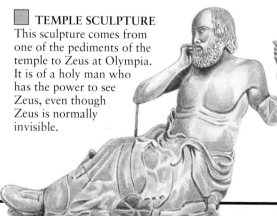

TEMPLE SCULPTURE
This sculpture comes from one of the pediments of the temple to Zeus at Olympia. It is of a holy man who has the power to see Zeus, even though Zeus is normally invisible.

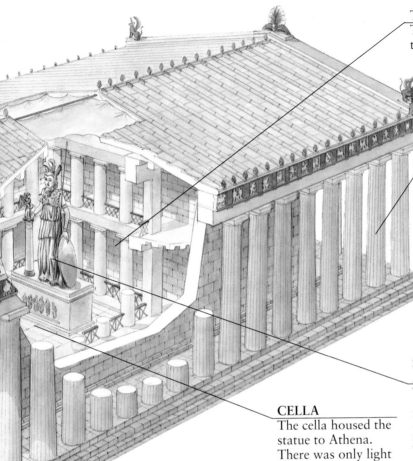

TREASURE STORE
The Athenians kept the money collected from cities in their empire inside the temple.

COLUMNS
Greek temples were always surrounded by columns. Those of the Parthenon were in the finest marble, brought from the nearby quarries of Pentele.

CELLA
The cella housed the statue to Athena. There was only light from one door so the statue must have looked rather frightening.

STATUE OF ATHENA
The massive statue of Athena in the Parthenon was sculpted by Phidias. The outside of the wooden statue was coated in gold, and Athena's skin was made of ivory.

FRIEZE
Greeks carved pictures on to their walls, called friezes. This one is on the inner wall of the Parthenon. It is the great procession of the Panathenaeic festival.

CARYATID PORCH
This porch, with its columns in the shape of women, was part of an ancient temple to Athena called the Erechtheion.

THE OLYMPIC GAMES

Every four years from 776 BC the cities of Greece forgot their quarrels and sent their best athletes to compete at games held in honour of Zeus at Olympia. Thousands of spectators came too. There were all kinds of running and horse races, and competitions. Although the prizes were only wreaths of olive branches there could be no greater honour than to win at Olympia and the winners were welcomed back with pride to their home cities.

CHARIOT RACING
The chariot race was the most dangerous Olympic event. The chariots had to race round a circuit several times and crashes were common.

STADIUM
At Olympia the running track was 192m long. Up to 40,000 spectators could sit on the low hills around it to watch the races. All the athletes ran naked.

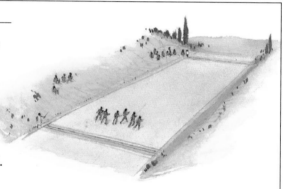

WRESTLING
Wrestling was popular and could be won by throwing your opponent three times, or by forcing him to surrender.

LOOK OUT FOR THESE

TEMPLE TO ZEUS
The great temple to Zeus at Olympia took ten years to build. It contained a massive statue of Zeus made by Phidias.

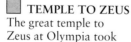

CHARIOTEER
This famous bronze statue of a charioteer was found at Delphi. Originally he drove a four-horse chariot. It was made to celebrate a victory by a Greek from Sicily in games held at Delphi. The statue was made up of several separate pieces of bronze.

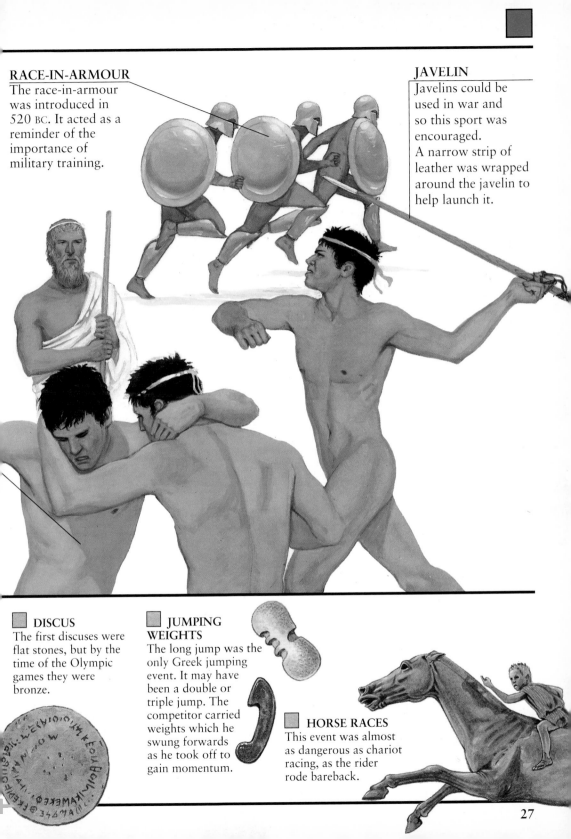

RACE-IN-ARMOUR
The race-in-armour was introduced in 520 BC. It acted as a reminder of the importance of military training.

JAVELIN
Javelins could be used in war and so this sport was encouraged.
A narrow strip of leather was wrapped around the javelin to help launch it.

DISCUS
The first discuses were flat stones, but by the time of the Olympic games they were bronze.

JUMPING WEIGHTS
The long jump was the only Greek jumping event. It may have been a double or triple jump. The competitor carried weights which he swung forwards as he took off to gain momentum.

HORSE RACES
This event was almost as dangerous as chariot racing, as the rider rode bareback.

THE FAMILY HOME

This is the house of a rich Greek family. It was built of mudbrick with small windows and a tiled roof. There was usually only one door. The furniture was very simple although some floors might have mosaics. Grain, oil and wine from the owner's farm were stored in the house.

In Athens, the women spent most of their lives in the home. There would be an open courtyard in the centre where they would work at their spinning and carry out other household jobs.

They would also cook with the help of slave girls.

Men spent most of their time outside the house. In the evenings they might bring men friends home for a meal but their wives and daughters were not allowed to join them.

BOARD GAMES
The Greeks had board games where a dice was thrown and counters moved. Children also played 'heads or tails' with pieces of painted pottery.

FAMILY ROOM
Hestia, the goddess of the home and family, watched over this room. Here mothers would play with their children around a fire lit in Hestia's honour.

KITCHEN
Cooking was done over an open fire in earthenware pots, often by slaves.

 LOOK OUT FOR THESE

POT
Simple unpainted pottery was used for storing wine and oil and fetching water. If there was no well in the house, women would fetch the water from a fountain.

 **STOOL**
Stools, like all furniture, were simple and wooden. In the richest homes furniture was decorated with gold and silver.

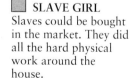 **SLAVE GIRL**
Slaves could be bought in the market. They did all the hard physical work around the house.

ALTAR AND COURTYARD
Every house would have its own altar in the courtyard. Sacrifices were made to favourite gods.

BEDROOM
Beds were covered with brightly coloured blankets. Clothes were stored in chests.

MEN EATING
Men would lie on couches to eat. Their food would be served by slave girls.

CHILD'S RATTLE
Children were given pottery toys. This pig is a rattle. Children also had dolls and tops.

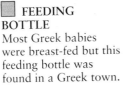

FEEDING BOTTLE
Most Greek babies were breast-fed but this feeding bottle was found in a Greek town.

HESTIA
Hestia was the goddess of the home and family. Any new arrival in the family – a baby, a bride or a slave – was walked around the fire lit in her honour to receive Hestia's protection.

GREEK WOMEN

Women married when they were about 15. Their husbands were usually in their twenties. Marriages were arranged between families, and when everything had been agreed the bride was taken in a procession to her new home. Once her first child had been born, she was seen as a full member of her new family.

The wife looked after everything in the new home, including the young children. In richer homes she would have slaves to help her. However, in poorer families she would be not much better than a slave as all the household tasks had to be done by hand.

Couples could get divorced, but few wives would have been able to afford to leave their husbands.

BRIDE
The bride remained veiled until she had arrived at her new home and had been welcomed to the household. The couple was showered with nuts and dried fruit for good luck.

PROCESSION
After a wedding feast at the bride's house, the bridegroom would take her back to his house. The procession took place at night, with music and hymns.

RITUAL BATH
Before her wedding the bride had a bath in water drawn from a holy spring. It marked the beginning of her new life.

LOOK OUT FOR THESE

MIRROR COVER
Mirrors were made of polished bronze. This mirror cover shows Aphrodite, goddess of love, and Eros, the boy god of love.

LOUTROPHOUS
The loutrophous was a special ceremonial vase which carried the water used for the bride's ritual bath. The bride might offer a small vase to the gods either at the time of her engagement or after she was married.

BEST FRIEND

The bridegroom would select one of his closest friends to travel in the procession cart with him and his bride.

MOTHER OF THE GROOM

The bridegroom's mother would be at the door of her son's home to welcome the new bride.

 EARRING

This beautifully made gold earring came from one of the wealthy Greek cities of southern Italy.

WOMEN IN BAKERY

This statue shows women preparing loaves in a bakery. Greeks hated being the servants of others. Wherever possible they would use foreigners or slaves for jobs such as these.

LEKYTHOS

A lekythos was a pot used for holding perfumed oil. The oil would be sprinkled on after a bath. Here again the painting is of the goddess Aphrodite.

EDUCATION

School was only for boys. They began school at the age of seven. The main subjects were reading, writing and music. The Greeks loved music. It was important to learn to play well as music was part of every festival and celebration. Often a schoolroom would also have a palaistra – a training ground for physical education – next door.

In Athens it was important to read because the laws were written out in stone. Children also learned to read the work of great poets like Homer. Writing was done on a wax tablet which could be smoothed over and written on again.

A few girls learned to read but most were only taught how to look after a home.

PHYSICAL EDUCATION
The Greeks valued fitness and skill at sport. Boys learned the sports of the Olympic games in a palaistra, a training area such as the one above. Well-trained boys were also useful as soldiers. Boys always exercised naked.

LOOK OUT FOR THESE

INSCRIPTION
Important laws would be engraved on stone for everyone to read. The words were written without spaces between them and with no punctuation.

LYRE
An educated man was supposed to be able to play the lyre. The lyre would be made from a tortoiseshell covered on its hollow side by an ox skin. It was used to accompany songs and poetry, especially at evening drinking parties.

READING OUT LOUD

This boy is reading out loud to his teacher. Large amounts of poetry were learnt by heart.

TEACHERS

There were different teachers for music, reading and sport. Teachers were not well paid and therefore teaching was not a popular profession.

PUPILS

These pupils are writing on their wax tablets. The same word was practised many times.

◼ READING A SCROLL

The papyrus plant from Egypt was made into paper. It was rolled up in a scroll.

◼ PIPES

Pipes were made of wood or bone. It was normal to play two at the same time. Musicians competed at games and festivals. The band round this player's head shows he has won one of these competitions.

◼ KITHARA

This was a particularly grand form of lyre used at the big music festivals.

SYMPOSIUM

In the evening the richer men would meet for a drinking party known as a symposium. There would be up to 15 guests. They would lie down on couches. Often they decorated their heads with flowers.

For food there might be fish and meat, vegetables, and bread made from wheat. This was much better than the normal diet of barley bread and olive oil. Wine was always drunk mixed with water. The finest Greek pottery was used at the symposium.

Later in the evening there would be music and dancing. The guests would compete with each other in singing or playing the lyre. They might also recite poetry. One game, called kottabos, involved flicking wine from a cup at a target.

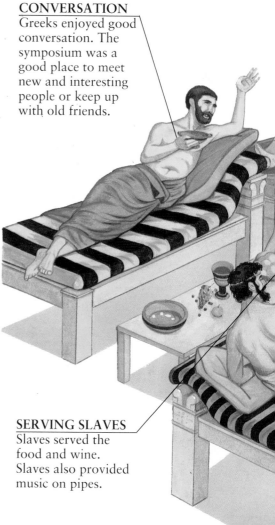

CONVERSATION
Greeks enjoyed good conversation. The symposium was a good place to meet new and interesting people or keep up with old friends.

SERVING SLAVES
Slaves served the food and wine. Slaves also provided music on pipes.

 LOOK OUT FOR THESE

KRATER
The krater was the large pot in which the wine and water were mixed. The mixing was always done by the host of the party. Unmixed wine was supposed to be bad for you.

OINOCHOE
After the wine was mixed it was put into a jug, an oinochoe, and was poured into cups.

FOOD
Greek food was simple. There might be a plate of fish and vegetables, such as leeks and onions, followed by apples, cheese and honey cakes.

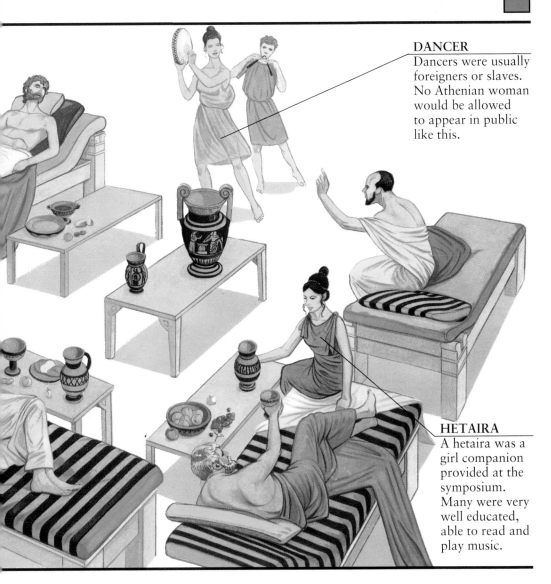

DANCER
Dancers were usually foreigners or slaves. No Athenian woman would be allowed to appear in public like this.

HETAIRA
A hetaira was a girl companion provided at the symposium. Many were very well educated, able to read and play music.

 OIL LAMP
Lamps such as these were filled with oil. A wick was placed in the spout and then lit.

DRUNKEN BRAWL
Guests were not supposed to get drunk at a symposium.

However, it certainly did happen as this picture shows.

PAN PIPES
Pan pipes were named after Pan, a god of shepherds and flocks. He was said to have invented the pipes.

THEATRES AND ACTORS

The Greeks were the first people to have theatres. Plays were held at the great religious festivals with different writers competing with each other for a prize. The theatres were built into a hillside and the audience could hear every word from the stage. The actors always wore masks and dressed up to show what character they were pretending to be.

A chorus would stand in an area in front of the stage, or proscenium, called the orchestra. Plays were either tragedies or comedies.

AUDITORIUM
The audience might come from all over Greece. They would sit on stone steps in the auditorium. A large auditorium seated up to 14,000 people.

MASQUERADE
Not all plays were serious. Often the actors would dress up as animals and put on a comedy show. The 'animals' would dance to music.

LOOK OUT FOR THESE

TICKETS
These are the theatre tickets. The letters would tell you where to sit. At big festivals the theatre would be packed out.

MASK
All actors wore masks and the audience would recognise a king or a messenger immediately. This mask would have been used for a character in a tragedy. The actors would have to speak loudly to be heard.

CHORUS

All plays had a chorus of up to 15 actors who stood in the orchestra. They chanted songs or told the background to the story.

ACTORS

There were usually no more than three actors on stage. They would act on a low stage behind the orchestra. Actors were always men.

◼ COMIC FIGURINES

Greeks enjoyed having comic figures in their plays. They were often slaves or servants and were given funny masks and padded clothes.

◼ ACTORS PREPARING

This actor has the mask of Dionysus, the god of wine, ready to put on. The other actor is a member of the chorus. He is already wearing a mask of a woman.

CRAFTSMEN

The Greeks were skilled craftsmen. Their pottery and sculpture is among the finest ever made. The Greeks learned many of their skills from the east but they always developed their own styles. Craftsmen were proud of their work and would often sign it with their own name.

Most Greek craftsmen had their own workshop with perhaps one or two slaves to help them. Tools were very simple and everything had to be made by hand. Each type of craft had its own corner of a city. For example, 200 potters and painters worked together in the same area of Athens.

The god of craftsmen, particularly those using fire, was Hephaestus. He had a fine temple in Athens overlooking the blacksmiths' workshops.

ARMOURER

Helmets were hammered out of one sheet of bronze. A leather cap was fitted inside. Great skill was needed to make a helmet fit well.

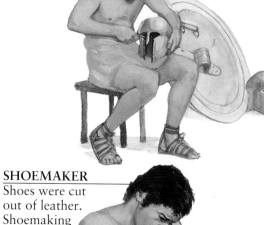

SHOEMAKER

Shoes were cut out of leather. Shoemaking was one of the least respected crafts.

LOOK OUT FOR THESE

KORAI

Figures were made as memorials to the dead or offerings to the gods. This statue has the headdress of a priestess. Female statues (korai) were always clothed.

NECKLACE

The finest gold workers were those of the city of Taras in southern Italy, where this necklace comes from.

IRON WORKERS

Iron was the commonest metal. It was used to make weapons and simple tools for farm work. It was melted in a furnace so it could be hammered into shape.

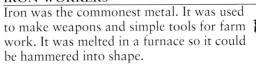

POTTER

Athenian pots were the best in the world. They were usually decorated with pictures of heroes and their adventures.

SCULPTOR

The Greek sculptors were brilliant at creating lifelike figures and reliefs. It might take six months to carve a single statue.

MARBLE HEAD

This marble head was found in Athens. It is believed to be of Poseidon, god of the sea.

STATUE

This bronze statue is of Zeus about to throw a thunderbolt. It was found in a shipwreck.

GEM

This flying heron is carved on chalcedony, a favourite stone for engravers. The name of the engraver, Dexamenos, is carved under the bird. Gems could be worn on fingers or at the end of necklaces.

LEARNING AND INVENTIONS

The Greeks had enormous curiosity. They liked to understand how things worked. Greek doctors would try to understand disease. Greek astronomers would observe the stars. Greek scientists, such as Aristotle and Archimedes, studied the world around them, and its animals, plants and different peoples. They recorded their ideas and laid down the foundations for modern maths and science.

Philosophers (lovers of wisdom) such as Plato and Socrates would ask questions like: 'What is a good man?' and 'Is there a best way to run a state?' They would argue about these problems in small groups. Luckily many of their discussions were written down and can still be read today.

ARCHIMEDES' SCREW

The Archimedes' screw lifted water by forcing it up a pipe. Archimedes designed it to pump water out of ships. Today it is still used to pump water out of streams for irrigating crops.

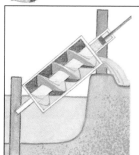

HOW IT WORKS

The end of the screw was placed in water. As it was turned, the water was forced upwards until it poured out at a higher level.

LOOK OUT FOR THESE

ARROW MACHINE

The 5th and 4th centuries BC were a time of war, with rival cities trying to conquer each other. Most new inventions were connected with warfare. This arrow machine was invented at Syracuse, a city well known for its attacks on others.

SIEGE MACHINE

Most Greek cities had strong walls around them. The only way to capture these cities was to make siege machines such as this one. The city was attacked by catapults from the top of the machine, or soldiers climbed up inside them and fought their way onto the city walls.

PHILOSOPHER TEACHES AT THE STOA

Philosophers would argue with small groups of students to try and find the truth about the problems that worried them. A common meeting place was a cool stoa such as this one.

SOCRATES
Socrates was one of the most famous philosophers. He was put to death for questioning belief in the gods.

ARISTOTLE
Aristotle, one of the first great scientists, wrote books on biology, astronomy, politics and maths.

ECLIPSE
Greek science is said to have begun in 585 BC when the philosopher Thales, from Miletus, correctly predicted an eclipse of the sun by the moon.

MATHEMATICS
Pythagoras is said to have discovered the famous theorem about the sides of a right angled triangle.

EARLY THEORIES OF ASTRONOMY
The Greeks believed that the earth was the centre of the universe. They were endlessly curious about the stars and put forward many theories about how they moved through the sky. These theories were believed for 1,500 years before later scientists disproved them.

ILLNESS AND DEATH

Life in Greece was certainly healthy for some. There are many examples of Greeks living to over 80 years old. But as there were no cures for simple childhood illnesses, many children died young.

Many people believed illnesses were caused by the gods and that prayers and sacrifices were important to prevent them.

There were also Greek doctors. They saw illness as the failure of the body to work properly. They examined the patient carefully and tried to work out what was the best cure. They understood that exercise, fresh air and eating the right food were important for good health. These doctors, such as Hippocrates, were the founders of modern medicine.

ASKLEPIOS
Asklepios was the god of healing. His temples could be found throughout the Greek world. Ill people would ask for his help.

LOOK OUT FOR THESE

WOMB

This model of a womb may have been made to thank a god for a safe pregnancy.

TOOLS
Greek doctors carried out simple operations. These are some of the instruments they used. Operations must have been very painful and the wounds must have often become infected causing the patient to die.

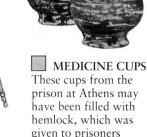

MEDICINE CUPS
These cups from the prison at Athens may have been filled with hemlock, which was given to prisoners condemned to die.

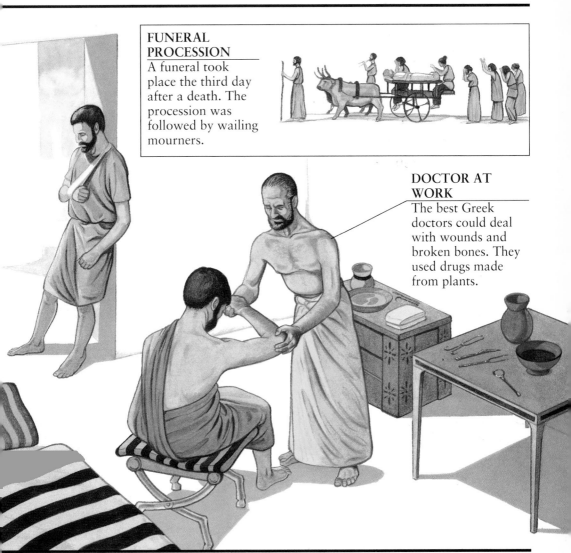

FUNERAL PROCESSION

A funeral took place the third day after a death. The procession was followed by wailing mourners.

DOCTOR AT WORK

The best Greek doctors could deal with wounds and broken bones. They used drugs made from plants.

▢ TOMBSTONE

The ashes of the dead were buried in a graveyard. Richer families would then set up a tombstone. This beautiful one shows a small girl with her doves. The family would visit once a year for special prayers. It was an important duty to tend the graves.

▢ TOMB

The richest families of all would have their own tombs. These would be decorated with pictures of dead members of the family. The grandest might be decorated inside with a mosaic floor.

GLOSSARY

Words in SMALL CAPITAL letters indicate a cross-reference.

acropolis The highest part of any Greek city, used by the city for defence or for placing its finest buildings.

Aegean Sea The sea between what is now Greece and Turkey. All the coasts around it were settled by Greeks.

agora The market place of a city.

Apollo One of the most popular of the Greek gods. He was god of healing, music and for consulting about the future.

archaeology Finding out about the past by discovering and examining what has survived.

Archimedes Greek scientist, remembered for the invention of the Archimedes' screw.

Aristotle One of the world's first great scientists. He taught in Athens in the 4th century BC.

Asklepios The god of healing.

Assembly The 'parliament' of Athens or any other Greek city, where its CITIZENS would meet to discuss their affairs.

Athena A goddess of war who was also the special protector of the city of Athens.

capital The carved stone on top of a column. The style in which a capital was carved would vary from one part of Greece to another.

chorus A group of actors who would chant songs or fill in the background to a play.

citadel A fortified hill top from which the surrounding countryside was ruled.

citizen A member of a city. In Athens citizenship was restricted to those born in the city to parents who were both citizens. Only male citizens could join in the city's affairs.

Delphi The home of a famous ORACLE of APOLLO.

democracy A system of government where the people make their own decisions about their city's or country's affairs. The Athenians were the first people to use democracy.

Etruscans A people of Italy with whom the Greeks traded. They provided iron and took the finest of the Greek pottery.

Hera The goddess of marriage and married women, the wife of ZEUS.

Hestia The goddess of the home and the family.

Homer The greatest of the Greek poets.The stories of the *Iliad* and the *Odyssey* had existed for hundreds of years. He wrote them as poems in about 700 BC.

hoplite A Greek foot soldier. He would be armed with a spear and sword and protected by a shield.

juror Jurors listened to criminal cases and decided whether the accused was guilty or innocent. In Athens any male CITIZEN could become a juror.

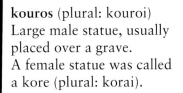

kouros (plural: kouroi) Large male statue, usually placed over a grave. A female statue was called a kore (plural: korai).

krater A large pot in which wine and water would be mixed before drinking.

Linear B The script used by the MYCENAEANS. The language used in Linear B is an early form of Greek.

lyre The most popular form of musical instrument in Greece. Poetry would be recited or songs sung to the lyre.

marble A hard stone, usually white, which was used in the finest Greek buildings.

Mount Olympus A mountain in northern Greece where the Greeks believed that the gods lived.

Mycenaeans The first Greeks, a warrior people named after one of their cities, Mycenae.

Naucratis An important Greek trading post in Egypt. The Greeks traded silver for Egyptian corn.

Olympic Games Games held every four years at Olympia, competed in by athletes from all over the Greek world.

oracle A message from a god or goddess giving advice, or prophesying. The Greeks would go to a temple to ask their question. A priest or priestess would relate the god's or goddess's answer. The most famous oracle was that of the god APOLLO at DELPHI.

orchestra A circular space in a theatre between the stage and the audience. The CHORUS would stand here.

palaistra A training ground for sports, such as wrestling.

Parthenon The greatest temple of Athens, built on the ACROPOLIS in honour of ATHENA.

pediment The triangular piece of stone at the end of the roof of a temple. It was usually carved with statues of the gods.

Pericles The leading statesman of Athens in the 5th century BC.

phalanx The HOPLITES would fight together in rows, one behind the other. The whole group was known as a phalanx.

Phoenicians A seafaring people from the eastern Mediterranean who were great rivals of the Greeks.

Plato The greatest of the Greek philosophers. He taught in Athens in the 4th century BC.

sacrifice A ceremony that involved killing animals and offering them to the gods. The Greeks believed the support of the gods could be gained by this.

Socrates A famous Athenian philosopher who was put to death for questioning belief in the gods.

stoa A long building of two storeys. The ground floor was left open and people could talk or do business together out of the heat of the sun.

trireme The Greek warship.

Zeus The father of the gods; god of the sky and storms.